ADVANCE PURRS FOR

HISTORICAL
CATS

"Scariest book I've ever read!"

—STEPHEN KING'S CAT

"I laughed, I cried, I got very depressed, I napped."

—WILLIAM STYRON'S CAT

"I didn't understand it. It was much too complicated for me."

—STEPHEN HAWKING'S CAT,
author of *A Brief History of Pounce* ™

"Perfect for ripping out the pages and using them as doilies. They're the exact size of a supper dish."

—MARTHA STEWART'S CAT

"The tension was unbearable. The final trial scene was so graphic and realistic, I could barely put this extraordinary book down to go eat. But, of course, I did."

—JOHN GRISHAM'S CAT

"Accessible, important, historically accurate, and it rights a lot of crucial wrongs. Best of all, it's perfect for lying on when your human is trying to read it."

—DANIEL BOORSTIN'S CAT

"I won't rest until I find out who 'Norton' really is. He's clearly an insider who has spent much time with real cats on the Feline Beltway. My guess is that he actually *is* a cat. But what's clear is he knows whereof he meows."

—ANONYMOUS'S CAT

"The account of familial hissing and scratching stings with the kind of honesty we haven't seen since Thomas Wolfe's cat's classic *Look Homeward, Cutesy-Pie.* The portrayal of a tabby struggling against his roots glitters with a sweet, uncomplicated craziness that grips and moves and makes you want to climb a tree and never come down. If I didn't still have my claws, I would applaud this masterpiece."

—PAT CONROY'S CAT

"I loved the fight scenes. I think I'll write six books about cats in the next three weeks and get them all published to great acclaim."

—JOYCE CAROL OATES'S CAT

"My editor said I have to write this blurb myself. Fine, I said, I can do that. And I will. Just as soon as I get paid. No problem. I'll write a lusty, sexy blurb and I dare anyone to say it's trashy! Go ahead! I'll sue the pants off you! Get it? Sue the pants off you? See? It really is sexy. Who said writing is hard? Can a publisher reject a blurb?

—JOAN COLLINS'S CAT

HISTORICAL
CATS

by
Norton, the Cat Who Went to Paris
with
Peter Gethers & Norman Stiles
Illustrations by William Bramhall

A JANIS A. DONNAUD & ASSOCIATES, INC. BOOK

FAWCETT COLUMBINE
NEW YORK

To Laura, who is now with God's cat

And to Gazzi, my new pal, and
Tate, for being such a good agent's cat

Introduction
by
Norton,
The Cat Who Went to Paris

This was not an easy book to write. Let's face it—no book is easy to write when you don't have opposable thumbs.

Living in semiretirement after my last book tour, I suppose I could have been content to spend the rest of my nine lives in the lap of luxury (and I mean that literally; my human has an extremely comfortable lap). However, on my many travels around the world, I did not merely dine out in fancy restaurants and act cute on airplanes, despite the distortions written about me by my so-called owner in *The Cat Who Went to Paris* and *A Cat Abroad.* In my free time, I didn't just curl up *on* a few books, I curled up *with* a few books. And what I read really began to make my fur stand on end. Ever since I was a kitten riding around town in my human's pocket, I was a history buff. Now, as I began to leap up onto library shelves in search of feline facts, I found a void. A wasteland. An endless litter box in which the history of an entire species seemed to have been buried.

While there are countless numbers of books on Thomas Jefferson, where is the book on Thomas Jefferson's cat? Why are his once magnificent catnip gardens no longer found at Monticello? And where do you think Jefferson got the idea for independence in the first place? While we're on the subject, how is it possible that so little is known about Søren Kierkegaard's cat, who developed the brilliant philosophy that all dogs are merely a figment of the imagination? Why is there no monument to Ernest Hemingway's cat, who wrote the classic *A Farewell to Mice*? Or to Joe DiMaggio's cat, who not only ate sliced chicken in gravy fifty-six days in a row, but was married to Marilyn Monroe's cat? The answer, my friends, is *catism*. But the fact that cats have been at the center of all historical events since the beginning of time—remember Adam and Eve's cat, Ribs?—is a secret that can no longer be kept. *Must* no longer be kept.

Thus, this book. My collaborators and I have attempted to right the wrongs of history. We have scoured the world in search of rare manuscripts; we have conducted thousands of interviews and skritched hundreds of bellies in an attempt to get information. I apologize for any omissions, but if there are any errors, I can only claim *meowa culpa*. If it is true that behind every great man there is a great woman, then it is even truer that behind every great human there is an even greater cat. I just hope that our research and our passion can, at long last, bring that fact forth to the world at large.

Norton
Sag Harbor, New York
1996

HISTORICAL
CATS

Nathan Hale's Cat

"I only regret that I have but nine lives
to give for my country."

ALBERT EINSTEIN'S CAT

Ran around the living room at the speed of
light for no reason at all, relatively speaking.

SIGMUND FREUD'S CAT

Discovered that the primary motivating
factor behind all behavior is the urge to rub
up against furniture.

PAINTING BY REMBRANDT'S CAT

Aristotle's Cat Contemplating the
Bust of Homer's Cat

MOSES'S CAT

Carried down the 11th Commandment
from mountaintop: "Thou Shalt Not Eat the
Same Food Two Days in a Row."

NEIL ARMSTRONG'S CAT

First cat to set foot on a freshly shellacked
living room floor. Uttered the immortal
words: "That's one small step for a cat, one
giant leap onto the credenza."

MICHAEL JACKSON'S CAT

After having plastic surgery to make
him look like Diana Ross's cat.

G. Gordon Liddy's Cat
B. Bootsy Liddy

Set fire to his own tail just for the fun of it.

VINCE LOMBARDI'S CAT

"Scratching the most expensive furniture
isn't everything. It's the *only* thing."

FDR's Cat

"We have nothing to fear
but the dog next door."

NAPOLEON'S CAT

Exiled to bathroom after throwing up
on Decree of Fontainebleau.

MALCOLM X'S CAT

Muffin X

Marie Antoinette's Cat

"Let them eat dry food."

KARL MARX'S CAT

"Dogs are the opium of the people."

Jerry Garcia's Cat

"What a long, strange nap it's been."

MEOWSHE DAYAN

Yassir Aracat

ALBERT CAMUS'S CAT

Wrote quintessential existential novel,
The Strange Dog.

Isaac Newton's Cat

Discovered gravity while falling out
of an apple tree.

Norton's Timeline of Historical Cats

King Tut wrapped for mummification; one day later, his cat, Prince Tootie, removes wrapping and carries it to top of Cheops Pyramid at Giza

Hippocrates, "Father of Medicine," born

Plato's cat becomes pupil of Socrates's cat

B.C.

| 20,000 | 1352 | 901 | 460 | 440 | 407 | 405 |

Andrew Lloyd Webber's ancestor, Thorg Lloyd Webber, draws 1st cave painting of cat

Israelites start collection of Solomon's sayings; Solomon's cat starts collection of Solomon's shoelaces

Hippocrates's cat, Meowcrates, breaks 1st medicine bottle while jumping on 1st medicine cabinet

Catapult first used successfull by Spartan soldiers

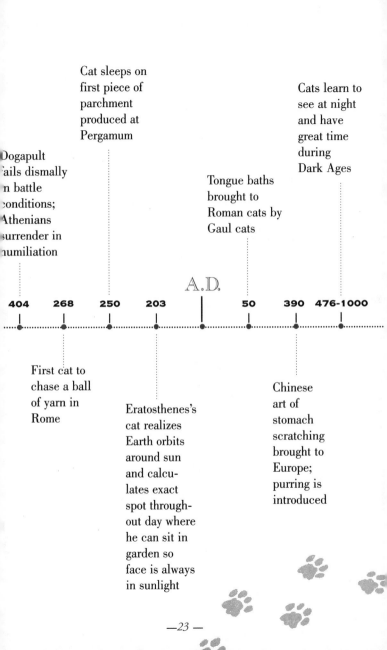

Cat sleeps on first piece of parchment produced at Pergamum

Cats learn to see at night and have great time during Dark Ages

Dogapult fails dismally in battle conditions; Athenians surrender in humiliation

Tongue baths brought to Roman cats by Gaul cats

A.D.

404   268   250   203   50   390   476-1000

First cat to chase a ball of yarn in Rome

Eratosthenes's cat realizes Earth orbits around sun and calculates exact spot throughout day where he can sit in garden so face is always in sunlight

Chinese art of stomach scratching brought to Europe; purring is introduced

Ponce de León's Cat

POUNCE DE LEÓN

Discovered the Fountain of Catnip.

DR. KEVORKIAN'S CAT

Helped a neighbor's cat
commit suicide 9 times.

W. B. Yeats's Cat

Author of classic poem
Leda Ate the Swan.

STEVEN SPIELBERG'S CAT

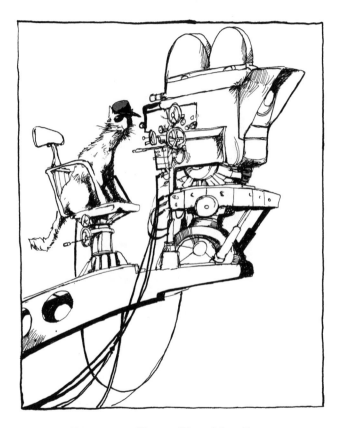

Director of box office hits *Paws*,
The Collar Purple,
and the groundbreaking *Puffy's List*.

Billy the Kid's Cat

BUBBA THE KITTEN

RICHARD NIXON'S CAT

Trixie

Patriotically accepted top-secret assignment
to play with 18 minutes of audiotape.

Babe Ruth's Cat

Knocked 714 pencils off desktop.

CHARLES DE GAULLE'S CAT

Celebrated the liberation of France
by eating chocolate mouse.

D.H. Lawrence's Cat

Wrote classic novel of love and hunger,
Lady Chatterley's Liver.

BETTY FORD'S CAT

Bootsy

Founded Bootsy Ford's Clinic
for Catnip Abusers.

Norton's Timeline of Historical Cats

Dutch invent fisherman's netting; Dutch cat named Gouda first to get entangled while trying to steal sardine

Christopher Columbus's cat catches first mouse in New World

Joan of Arc's cat captured by Burgundians while napping at Compiègne

John Smith's cat falls in love with Pocahontas's cat, Pookiehontas

1416 1429 1430 1431 1492 1515 1613 1657

Joan of Arc's cat naps throughout entire Siege of Orléans

Joan of Arc's cat naps while being burned at stake in Rouen

Monsieur Fromage, a French cat, shreds first factory-made tapestry at château in Loire

Zuzu, another French ca shreds firs factory-ma stocking i Paris

obert
ooke
vents the
alance
pring for
atches; his
at knocks
under the
ofa

John Milton
writes
Paradise Lost

Johann
Sebastian
Bach creates
Mass in B
minor; Bach's
cat creates
minor mess
in kitchen

Simón Bolívar
becomes
dictator of
Venezuela; still
can't get his cat to
eat canned tuna

1658	1664	1665	1701	1733	1773	1824	1852

ohn Milton's cat
oses pair of dice
nder bed

Charles XII
of Sweden
invades
Poland; his
neighbor,
Inga, feeds
the cat

The day after
the Boston Tea
Party, Paul
Revere's cat,
Churchie,
hisses at owner
when she
discovers
there's no
leftover ribbon
or wrapping
paper to play
with

Duke of
Wellington
dies; his cat,
"Biff"
Wellington,
moves in
with Earl of
Sandwich

CHAIRMAN MAO'S CAT'S
LITTLE RED LITTER BOX

Anastasia's Cat

Thought to have escaped Russia during
Revolution of 1917. Found hiding in Stalin's
closet in Kremlin in 1938.

PLATO'S CAT

Theorized that all life is merely a physical
reflection of our subjective imagination,
thus it is doubly important to clean
ourselves as often as possible.

THE ARTIST FORMERLY KNOWN AS PRINCE'S CAT

The Cat Formerly Known as
Peanut Butter

GEOFFREY CHAUCER'S CAT

Author of *The Canterbury Tails*.
Most famous creation is
The Cat Whose Wife Wouldn't Take a Bath.

EVA PERÓN'S CAT

"Don't meow for me, Argentina."

ANDY WARHOL'S CAT

Pop

PABLO PICASSO'S CAT

Accidentally ran into window
and created cubism.

FERDINAND MAGELLAN'S CAT

First cat to circumnavigate
the upstairs bedroom.

Barbra Streisand's Cat

Won Oscar for *Funny Fur*.
Still never gets the recognition she deserves
for all the cute things she does.

René Descartes's Cat

"I think I'm cute, therefore I am."

COPERNICUS'S CAT

Published *Commentnapiolus*, in which he
stated it's great to sleep in the sun.

OLIVER STONE'S CAT

Directed controversial film *Morris*,
which claims the famous feline didn't die
of natural causes but was assassinated by
rogue elements within the SPCA.

Victor Hugo's Cats

Wrote *Les Misérables*, the story of
two poor French cats whose humans disappeared
for "le weekend" and only left them dry food.

BEETHOVEN'S CAT

In spite of the fact that he was deaf,
was able to meow at such an annoying
pitch that Beethoven was evicted
from his apartment.

LEO TOLSTOY'S CAT

Wrote first novel of social realism,
War and a Piece of Fish.

Fyodor Dostoyevsky's Cat

Wrote *Crime and Punishment and Do It Again Anyway*, complex novel about an evil Russian Blue, Raskolnikat, who eats off his owner's plate despite many stern warnings. Raskolnikat has overwhelming feelings of guilt but looks so cute he is never punished and ultimately dies weighing 57 pounds.

TENNESSEE WILLIAMS'S CAT
BIG DADDY

Filed landmark lawsuit after paws were permanently
damaged on owner's hot tin roof.

MARK TWAIN'S CAT

Author of *A Connecticut Cat in
King Arthur's Hamper.*

Norton's Timeline of Historical Cats

Nietzsche
publishes
*Thus Spake
Zarathustra*;
Nietzsche's cat
publishes
*Thus Meowed
Tabbythustra*

James Joyce's
cat, Ulysses,
publishes
*Portrait of the
Mouser as a
Young Cat*

"You're the
Cream in My
Coffee" hits
pop charts;
"You're the
Cream in My
Saucer" hits
cat charts

Jean-Paul
Sartre's cat
can't find
way out of
Paris attic;
Sartre writes
No Exit

| 1892 | 1908 | 1916 | 1926 | 1928 | 1943 | 1944 | 194 |

W. G. Grace ends his
cricket career having
scored 54,000 runs; his
cat chases a cricket around
the room 54,000 times

Bob Hope's
cat chooses
"Manx for the
Memories" as
his theme
song

Pandit Neh
becomes
prime mini
of India; st
can't get ca
eat leftover
chicken tik

Hirohito becomes
emperor of Japan;
still can't get his
cat to eat canned
turkey bits

Ralph Nader publishes *Unsafe at Any Speed* about automobiles; his cat writes *Unsafe at Any Breed* about dogs

oger Bannister ns a mile in minutes 59 sec-nds; his cat runs p a bannister in seconds

Georges Pompidou becomes president of France; still can't get cat to eat day-old foie gras

| 1954 | 1954 | 1965 | 1965 | 1968 | 1969 | 1971 | 1974 |

Ernest Hemingway wins Nobel Prize for Literature; his cat, Shotgun, wins Nobel Prize for Litter

Broadway rock musical *Hair* opens; cat rock musical *Hairball* opens

TV series *Lassie* canceled

World premiere of classic film *Cat Ballou*

Patty Hearst kidnapped by Symbionese Liberation Army; neighbor feeds her cat for next 10 months

ALEXANDER GRAHAM BELL'S CAT

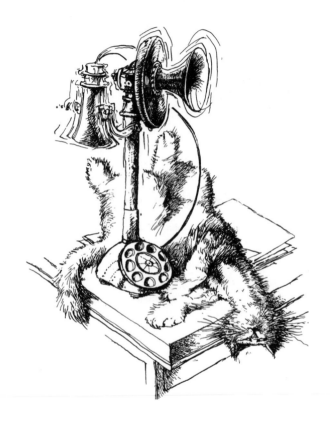

Made history for refusing
to come when called.

Prince Charles's Cat

LEONARD NIMOY'S CAT

"Live long and prosper and jump on your
human's head in the morning."

Madonna's Cat

Recorded top-selling feline single
of all time, "Like a Sturgeon."

Vincent van Gogh's Cat

Went into frenzy one starry night in
potato field in Arles and licked
off his own ear.

Brigitte Bardot's Cat

The original sex kitten.

DON KING'S CAT

Cat-fight promoter. Sent to the
pound for embezzling all of Mike Tyson's
cat's kibble.

Calamity Jane's Cat

CATASTROPHE JOAN

Clumsiest cat in Old West.
Once knocked over entire chuck wagon.

LOUIS PASTEUR'S CAT

Ran away from home after owner
insisted on using *his* milk for
some stupid experiment.

F. SCOTT FITZGERALD'S CAT

Wrote Great American Novel,
The Great Catsby.

STEPHEN SONDHEIM'S CAT

Composed classic tune "Send in the Birds."

William Shakespeare's Cat

Rosencrantz

While playing in garden, couldn't decide
if it was two bees or not two bees. It was.
Got stung twice on nose.

Clint Eastwood's Cat

"Make my supper!"

JULIUS CAESAR'S CAT

"Et tu, Fluffy?"

Liza Minnelli's Cat

Fifi with an F

NERO'S CAT

Fiddled with his tail while
Rome burned.

Norton's Timeline of Historical Cats

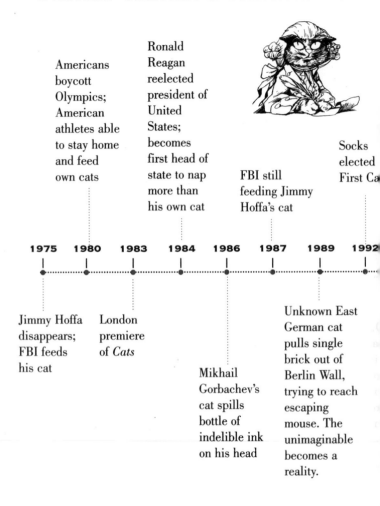

Americans boycott Olympics; American athletes able to stay home and feed own cats

Ronald Reagan reelected president of United States; becomes first head of state to nap more than his own cat

FBI still feeding Jimmy Hoffa's cat

Socks elected First Ca[

1975 1980 1983 1984 1986 1987 1989 1992

Jimmy Hoffa disappears; FBI feeds his cat

London premiere of *Cats*

Mikhail Gorbachev's cat spills bottle of indelible ink on his head

Unknown East German cat pulls single brick out of Berlin Wall, trying to reach escaping mouse. The unimaginable becomes a reality.

O.J.'s cat accused of eating mouse-guest; acquitted when close friend, Catto Kaelin, provides alibi

Norton wins Nobel Prize for Literature

"Historical Cats: The Miniseries" wins Emmy

1994   **1995**   **1996**   **1997**   **1998**   **1999**   **2000**

O.J. Simpson's cat generously gives extra room in mansion to freeloading mouse-guest

Historical Cats wins Pulitzer Prize

Historical Cats: The Movie wins Academy Award; *Historical Cats II* goes into pre-production

Andrew Lloyd Webber's new Broadway musical *Historical Cats!* wins Tony

Sir Edmund Hillary's Cat

Climbed highest telephone pole in Himalayas.
Took three weeks to remove his claws from back
of Sherpa fireman who brought him down.

JFK'S CAT

"Ask not what you can do for your human,
ask what your human can do for you."

LEONARDO DA VINCI'S CAT

Extraordinary Renaissance cat. Drew design for first mousetrap. Invented the scratching post. Conceived of first mechanical mouse.

Died before realizing his greatest dream—
the Cat Copter, which would allow cats to pursue
birds in flight.

HANS BRINKER'S CAT

Saved Holland when, while batting
tulip petal across cobblestone street,
accidentally got paw stuck in hole in dike.

ARNOLD SCHWARZENEGGER'S CAT

Strongest cat in history. Once carried Maria
Shriver's slipper from the bedroom to the
living room—while she was wearing it.

AL CAPONE'S CAT

Ate 14 mice on Valentine's Day, 1929.

J. Edgar Hoover's Cat

Ran Feline Bureau of Investigation for over forty years. Disgraced when discovered napping in one of his neighbor's dresses.

B. B. KING'S CAT
C. C. Queen

The food is gone
Bowl is empty as it can be
The food is gone, baby
Empty as a birdless tree
There ain't nothin' I can do
Except scratch up your
upholstery

The food is gone
The food is gone
You been away
For one whole day
Oh Lord, the food is gone

GEORGE WASHINGTON'S CAT

"I cannot tell a lie—
I coughed up the cherry pit in Martha's hat."